Miami. One o...
cities in the US has more th...
pastel-coloured Art Deco fa...

Its history is of booms and busts, reclaimed swamps, hurricanes, and crime waves. Throw in a diverse mix of communities and there's a rich panorama to explore.

The arrival of Art Basel turned Miami into a dynamic arts hub, with galleries regenerating Wynwood and now Little Haiti. Cocktail bars have exploded and the trashy South Beach scene of old has been turned on its head by fresh music venues.

Slow food pioneers have raised the dining level, but there's as much fun to be had exploring the street food scene—from Haitian seafood, Cuban sandwiches and Caribbean curries to Jewish delis and Argentine asado. In Miami you can eat something new three times a day, seven days a week.

Some local legends have shared their side of the city. A performative artist, an iconic Latin musician, a cocktail pioneer, and a bold, young curator. It's all about original minds and the creative vibe. Get lost in the sights, flavours and sounds of the city. Get lost in Miami.

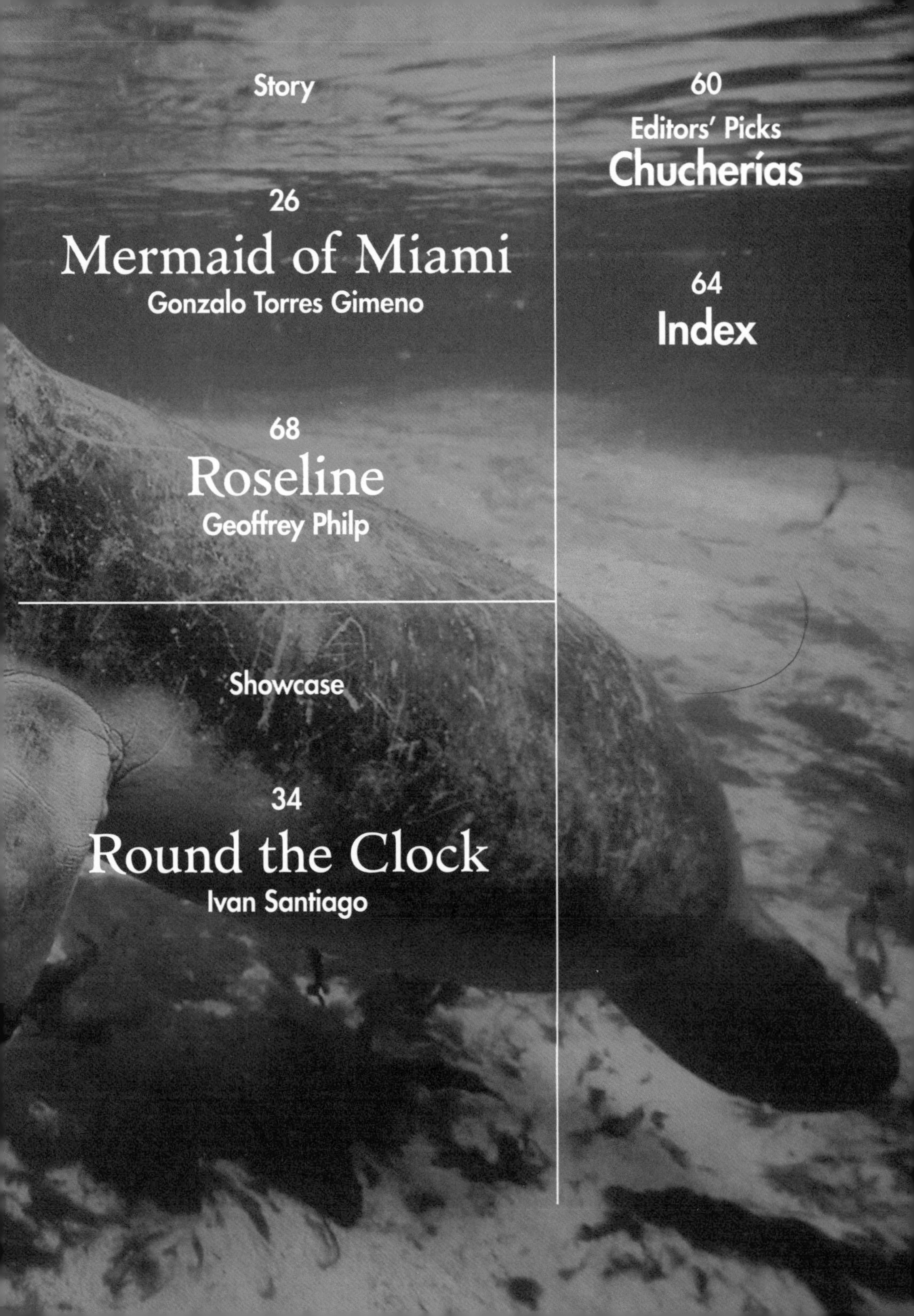

A modernist megalith of poured concrete, the *Miami Marine Stadium* was the first dedicated powerboat racing stadium in the US. If that's not impressive enough, it hosted concerts from the likes of Queen, Ray Charles and The Beach Boys. Public outcry saved it from planned demolition after Hurricane Andrew in 1992, and the abandoned structure has since been designated a local landmark.
• Miami Marine Stadium, Downtown, marinestadium.org

Make a Splash

The food and nightlife might be fantastic, but it's the turquoise waters that made Miami. The farther north, the more tranquil and family-friendly the beaches become, but South Beach offers top-notch people watching and the true vibe. The beautiful but tourist-ridden stretch of sand below 15th Street, with topless European jet setters and party promo parades, still holds a kernel of authenticity. But to splash with real Miamians, drop your flip flops in the sand around 3rd Street. You might score an invite to the evening's action— or to a friendly game of foot volley.
• 3rd Street, South Beach

From Carpark Fashion to Venezuelan Fusion

Tropical Ease

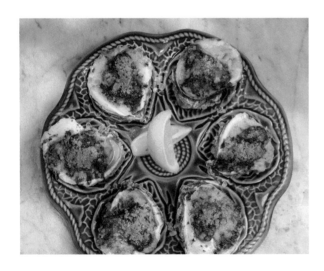

Food | Shell Game

It's all about glorious combinations at *Mignonette*—"Old Florida meets New Orleans" for décor, and "plain meets fancy" for cuisine. The day's oysters are posted on a giant marquee, providing inspiration—or torture—while you inevitably wait for a table in this former 1930s gas station. But don't stop at the aphrodisiac molluscs. A host of fish and seafood is offered—done in your choice of "plain" or "fancy"—with bisque, pies and plenty more. It's reasonably priced considering it all practically swam right in from the ocean.
• Mignonette, 210 NE 18th Street, Edgewater, mignonettemiami.com

Bayside Mode

Though not renowned for fashion, Miami has some new-generation mainstays. Luring big spenders into a carpark—not as dodgy as it sounds—is *Alchemist* (pictured; South Beach). If a four-figure Rodarte dress isn't on your list, catch the view from the breathtaking fifth floor. Multi-brand luxury store *The Webster* fronts South Beach, spanning three levels of curated garb, ranging from streetwear pros to classic brands. New girl on the retail block is 25-year-old fashion blogger Simonett Pereira and her store *Style Mafia* in Wynwood, catering to a smaller budget with a huge trend awareness. If your style defies "current season", discover vast stocks of vintage Gucci, Chanel and so on at North Miami's *C Madeleines*. Don't expect depreciation. Finally, consignment store *Fly Boutique* (Upper East Side) is more financially forgiving. Among pre-loved Dior gowns and Louis Vuitton luggage, find ornate homeware and larger furniture. Look out for the up-cycled creations of co-owner Jean Marie.

• Various locations, see Index, p. 64

It's not only the collection of more than 2,000 modern and contemporary art pieces—from Dan Flavin to Mark Handforth and Olafur Eliasson—that makes the *Pérez Art Museum Miami* worth a visit. The design of the complex by Pritzker Prize-winning architects Herzog and de Meuron is another powerful attraction. Combine your appreciation of PAMM's installations with a stroll through its Sculpture Garden, hosting works from Edgar Negret, Ernesto Neto, Jedd Novatt and Pablo Atchugarry. If you're spending a little more time in town, check specials such as top-class Art Talks or Poplife Social events on the third Thursday of every month. There are also concerts and DJ gigs to be enjoyed on the spectacular waterfront terrace—with a view as transcendent as the artwork.

• Pérez Art Museum Miami, 1103 Biscayne Boulevard, Downtown, pamm.org

Food | Steps to Heaven

Some say Uruguayan restaurant Parador La Huella—"huella" meaning "footprint"—is one of Latin America's finest. Surrounded by skyscrapers on Brickell Plaza, *Quinto La Huella* is its identical but shinier Miami twin. The centrepiece is a huge wood-fire parrilla where seafood and meat are grilled. And beside it, a sushi counter that doesn't forget its Latin heritage. Whether you come for the copious portions of the set lunch or an even more elaborate dinner, prepare to be blown away by a strong breeze of freshness.

• Quinto La Huella, 788 Brickell Plaza, Downtown, quintolahuella.com

Food · Night | **Se Baila Así**

Miami wears its huge Latin influence on its sleeve in Little Havana—more a way of life than a neighbourhood. Every year Calle Ocho—8th Street, by the way—hosts a carnival of culture. But every day is a unique parade of tastes, smells and sounds. *Cardón y El Tirano*'s explosive take on Venezuelan cuisine—think beef arepitas and plantain bombolini—will blow your palate. Aid digestion by shaking your tail at legendary music venue *Ball and Chain* (pictured), a former saloon where Billie Holiday dazzled guests in the 1950s. Or go informal at the 24/7 *Yambo*, a Nicaraguan restaurant-cum-theme park complete with gumball machine and kiddie horse ride. Try the potato-cheese "pescozones", or crunchy chicken tacos. A suitable stop en route home is at a Cuban café window for a final taste of magic.
• Little Havana, various locations, see Index p. 64

Culture | **Villa Real**

Imagine the sub-tropical lair of a Bond villain with a penchant for hallucinogens and antiques, and you might get close to the *Vizcaya Museum and Gardens*. Its interior is stuffed with precious objects—though a selection stolen in a notorious 1971 heist is still missing. The building is hewn out of Florida limestone and its eastside loggia is equipped with a giant telescope for viewing the bay. Meanwhile, the sprawling, Italian Renaissance-inspired gardens contain fountains, mazes and even a casino. Built in the early 20th century, the magnificent legacy of Chicago industrialist James Deering is a fascinating spot to visit—and Polaroid perfect for a golden sunset.
• Vizcaya Museum and Gardens, 3251 S Miami Avenue, vizcaya.org

"Let's drop everything and move to Miami", begged Jorge in his first big hit. And the move went better than he could have hoped. He's since landed multiple Grammy awards, and his singalong anthems are cherished by millions of people across Latin America

Jorge Villamizar, Musician

Comfort, Sea, Solitude

A slew of awards and hit records have made no dent in the Colombia-born musician's humility. From thirsty bike rides to the hottest stages, via fine Latin eating and short rib pasta, Jorge takes us on a lyrical tour of his Miami

What was your first view of Miami?

When I came in May 1992, I was coming from London. It was a big shock. May is already a hot month in Miami but coming into summer, I couldn't believe it. I'm from the Andes, so I've always lived in cold cities. To top it off, Hurricane Andrew hit September that year, so it was a real trial by fire. Besides the climate, what I was most impressed by was all the Latin, especially Cuban, culture. I didn't know any Cubans before and I had to learn how to understand them. The volume they speak at, the different accents, ideologies, migration waves... Apart from that, the solitude. This city makes me feel lonely. Later on I came to understand that it was a side-effect of this port of extreme materialism.

What neighbourhood do you live in?

I've lived all over, from South Beach to the Upper East Side— the coastal zone that faces the gulf. But I always return to Miami Beach—where I am now. Every area is like a different city. For example, when I lived in Normandy, I met an enormous Argentine community. It's come to be called Little Argentina. Meat, pasta, pizza and even Uruguayan chivitos. It's not glamorous, but populated by very charming, working-class people. I remember seeing barbecues on people's balconies, which would get you into trouble with neighbours and the fire department in any other part of town.

There's also an enormous Jewish community, many Orthodox Jews, synagogues, delis, beards, wigs. Fridays are nice because they don't drive, and they go out to temple in groups all dressed up. It gives the neighbourhood good energy.

A few blocks to South Beach, it's a totally different story. It's a sort of gay paradise. All these young people from the most repressive places suddenly come upon a world that not only tolerates them but promotes their lifestyle. They go out looking for fun with no fear. That openness generates a relaxed atmosphere attracting all types of bohemia. Besides, there are tons of modelling agencies, filling the streets with perfect men and women, right out of magazines. And of course, where there's beauty, there's money. The playboys in Ferraris and Lamborghinis aren't hard to find, nor the places where they can spend exorbitantly to demonstrate their status in this jungle.

On the mainland it's different. Cuban areas like Little Havana and the South West, or "Saguesera", have a different flavour. Things there are determined by the waves of Cuban migration that escaped Castro. But these are conservative people, marked by their disillusion with progressivism. They're white Caribbeans, working people, happy and proud of their Cuban origins. Those areas are filled with nostalgia for a lost world.

You tour a lot—what do you miss when you're not there? Such as food?

I travel a lot. I miss my kids above anything else. But also the city. Comfort, sea, solitude. I feel like I'm in space here. As for restaurants, *Salumeria 104*. Their pasta is amazing! Once in a while, when I deserve it, I treat myself. They make a very good botarga. And *Mandolin*, which makes great Greek and Turkish food.

There's a big difference between the US and Colombia in cooking, but Miami is a good solution. Where can we try authentic Latin flavours?

There's a little bit of everything in Miami! No question. It might

Named after Maradona's birthplace, Fiorito serves up an Argentine experience as authentic as Diego himself

hurt a few egos, but you can get food as good as in anybody's home country. Except for Mexican, which you can only get on the streets of Mexico. My favourite Colombian is *Monserrate*. The same with Peruvian cevicherías, Central American restaurants and Argentine asado—my favourite is *Fiorito* near the Design District. There's a French bakery ten blocks away called *Buena Vista Deli*—their croissants and quiche are to die for. And if I go to the movies on Lincoln Road, I stop by *Baires* for an empanada and a glass of wine.

Juices, something I miss from Colombia and Ecuador where I grew up, have gone through some weird changes here. Except for Cuban places like *El Palacio de los Jugos*, in Miami Beach you've got to resign yourself to the consumerist version. Juices in plastic bottles

preserved who knows how. But if you're riding your bike under the sun, there's not much of a choice.

Something that has changed for the worse is the decline of Cuban coffee culture. When I arrived you could find good coffee, made by little old Cubans on the corners. Little by little they disappeared. I miss 1990s cortados.

You're a family man now—what do you like to do with the little ones?

The French chocolateries here are spectacular. I share the chocolate vice with my children. *Beacon Hill Chocolates* makes great ice cream. For eating, Fiorito again. My kids think they're the owners there or something—all the waiters are their friends.

What are you favourite venues to play or listen to live music?

Hoy Como Ayer, in Little Havana, must be one of the best. Though I think in Miami it's more about the good musicians. My favourite is Michel Fragoso; an amazing Cuban pianist. He's a little crazy so you can't take him out of his element. You can find him in the *Tucán*, places on Calle Ocho like *Habana 305* or the lobby of *Soho House*, where he plays marvellously while the sophisticated tourists remain oblivious.

Miami has become a dance destination, but what about the singer-songwriters?
I like good DJs, I think they're also musicians, I don't mind the change as much. But the strongest singer-songwriter I've seen here is Jesse Jackson. A gringo that adores our Latin chaos and writes marvellous things—on the same level as any great writer right now.

Anywhere we'd never find you?
At night along Ocean Drive. Too much traffic, tourism, and muscular machos.

Where would you wish to go more?
The ones you can only reach by boat, somewhere with a good view or good wind. I still haven't forgiven myself for not having a sailboat, but easier said than done.

What would you tell an artist thinking of moving to Miami?
Electronic music is stronger and more interesting, but I'm too old to stay awake so I'm not well informed. Miami is a good home base for anyone trying to know Latin America from a musical standpoint. It's cheaper to fly from here to Latin cities than to fly between Latin cities. The US is still very innovative in terms of music and art. You can eat your chivito here, use your hi-speed internet, take a dip in the sea and then get on a cheap flight to see a show in New York or Nashville.

How do you see Miami in ten years?
Depends how much the sea level rises. I think that will affect us. But while it can, Miami will become a more important and rich city. It will continue to receive immigrants—now we're seeing more French and Russians arriving.

How could it welcome artists more?
I'm afraid for artists, because things are getting very expensive. We are not rich people. And if the beautiful areas become inaccessible for creatives, the vibe dies. Manhattan is dying. When the millionaires swoop in, it gets complicated. But there's still some space here. There's been a rise in population density—Brickell, Downtown, Midtown. This could generate interesting environments.

How do we have a good time when there isn't much of a budget?
Barbecues with friends. At the beach, in the beautiful parks. There are affordable restaurants all over.

And when there is?
Like in Vegas, "there's everything for your money". When I've got money to spare, I go to *Michael's Genuine* in the Design District, a modern American restaurant. Anything there with short ribs is good, even the short rib pasta! And the creamy chocolate dessert with olive oil and salt is a must.

Is Miami present in what you create?
It's fundamental. I'm completely Latin, but not from any one place. I've absorbed a lot from everyone—the ceviche, the asados, the feijoada—and of course the hamburgers and croissants.

Tuck into homespun Greek and Turkish food at Mandolin, an Aegean coastal tavern transplanted to the Design District

Fertile Ground

Where the roosters roam free, find a Caribbean feast for the senses and a colourful cultural hub. Welcome to the unexpected trip within your trip—no passport required

Shop | Voodoo That You Do

Indulge your esoteric side at any of the heavily perfumed "botanicas" peppering the area. Afro-Catholic syncretism was a combining of Christianity with the belief systems of Africans who came to the Americas as slaves. And saints, powders, oils and herbs related to this tradition line the walls of these stores, found all over Latin America and the US—and especially in Miami. Here, the botanicas vary in character: those in areas like Little Havana focus more on Afro-Cuban mythology, while Little Haiti's shops tend to cater to Santería and Yoruba needs. At *3×3 Santa Barbara Botanica*—going strong for over 15 years—you'll find something to scratch any mystical itch. Step into the elaborately stocked shop and let owner Laide Andre assist you in questions of the heart. This might include the occasional card-reading—or even help finding missing keys. Looking for love? There's a powder for that. Hungry for success? Take home a Ghede candle for good fortune. An assortment of figurines are available, with the Black Madonna—or Erzulie, to Haitian worshippers— a provocative memento for back home.
• 3×3 Santa Barbara Botánica, 5700 NE 2nd Avenue, Little Haiti

| Music Please

It was 1980 when Florence "Fi" Charles opened *Fifi Records*. And it's still the city's foremost spot for zouk or konpa—the popular music of Haiti—especially if you're seeking a rare 1970s or 1980s recording. And there's more: from soul to the latest fusion creole. Meanwhile, *Sweat Records* (pictured) caters for other musical tastes, acting as a nerve centre for the Miami indie scene. The used and new vinyl records, CDs, books and T-shirts reflect its quintessential spirit. And the in-house vegan coffee bar is a fine setting for some highly specific music chat.
• Little Haiti, various locations, see Index p. 64

Culture | New Territory

When developers sharked in on Miami's Wynwood area after it blossomed as an art hub, many galleries fled to Little Haiti. One space that led the charge was Gallery Diet—now re-named *Nina Johnson* after its curator. Johnson works closely with artists to tailor their work to the expansive space. And the shows tend to push boundaries, bleeding into other worlds like furniture design. The gallery has hosted the first show of filmmaker-artist Jonas Mekas—then aged 93—and the paintings of influential Brooklynite Seth Cameron, among others.
• Nina Johnson, 6315 NW 2nd Avenue, Little Haiti, ninajohnson.com

Food | Everything's All Right

This Neapolitan pizza joint wastes no time on an ultra-trendy interior, complicated menu or curated wine list. All energy is casually directed at being genuine. Take a seat outside and don't be shy of the mostly-Italian menu. It's hard to make a wrong order—the wood-fired pizzas are topped with a tomato sauce you wish you could bottle and there's no shortage of truffle oil on the appetisers. If you happen to avoid the Nutella pizza for dessert, do the right thing and get the affogato. For drinks? It's BYO with no corkage charge—a huge tick for everybody involved.
• Ironside Pizza, 7580 NE 4th Court, Little Haiti, pizzaironside.com

Get Your Jerk On

You can't get closer to the Caribbean on the US mainland than in Miami. But beside Cuba and Haiti, Jamaica also has its outposts in town, with Clive's Cafe its culinary embassy for almost 40 years. Start the day with ackee and saltfish. For lunch or dinner, classics like jerk chicken, curry goat and patties are nicely rounded off with home-made lemonade. Those wearing a Miami uniform like Gucci or Versace take note: this unpretentious spot tends to be clouded with a smoky haze from the grill.
• Clive's Cafe, 5890 NW 2nd Avenue, Little Haiti, clivescafe.com

Culture | Creator Curator

In 2005, Anthony Spinello started out as an art dealer by posting an ad on Craigslist. Within a year he'd garnered the attention of some of the biggest fish in the global pond. His gallery *Spinello Projects* has helped to launch numerous stars, including daring body artist Antonia Wright, self-taught painter Farley Aguilar and outdoor interventionist Agustina Woodgate. And all of them rave about the particular relationship they have with Spinello, as he pushes them onto wilder, greater things.
• Spinello Projects, 7221 NW 2nd Avenue, Little Haiti, spinelloprojects.com

Night | Rock Ain't Dead

You could chop off four fingers and still count the underground live music clubs worth mentioning in the Sunshine State on one hand. *Churchill's Pub* might even be the East Coast's most iconic remaining relic. Opened in 1979 and barely altered since then, the venue birthed the careers of Marilyn Manson and plenty more. Once've you made it past the painting of the British Bulldog himself, a large room for bands with a well-stocked bar and a couple of pool tables awaits. Breathe in the history, listen to whoever's on—and don't miss out on the sizable backyard.
• Churchill's Pub, 5501 NE 2nd Avenue, Little Haiti, churchillspub.com

Naomi vous invite — bon manger
650

Food | Spice of Life

When in Little Haiti, do as the Haitians do—get ready for a feast. A technicolour marlin in a red hat marks the spot at *Chef Creole*. Open your mind and palate to attractions like oxtail smothered in sauce and onions, and explosive barbecue pork and chicken. But the grail here is the seafood—battered, spiced and fried to perfection. Set your sights on the conch fritters, a Haitian specialty, and whole fried fish. These spoils are kept company by the holy Caribbean trinity of rice, beans and plantain. Everything is made to order, so settle down with an ice-cold Prestige beer for the wait. A more immersive experience awaits at

Naomi's Garden (pictured) The unofficial cultural centre for almost two decades recently revamped its garden, with space for konpa dance lessons, the occasional concert and, of course, al fresco dining. Naomi's grandson Naom uses less oil these days, resulting in a healthier take on the classics. At *Piman Bouk*, things are more intimate—and a lot more generous. Breakfast is no laughing matter—an order of grits-style polenta with beans will earn you an entire salad, plantain and maybe even the catch of the day. Come hungry and wash it down with a fresh tropical juice.

• Little Haiti, various locations, see Index p. 64

Renaissance Woman

One of Miami's most exciting young curators, Karla has spearheaded the regeneration of Little Haiti as an art hub—as she did with Wynwood before. She previously worked with Innocence Project—helping victims of wrongful convictions. No wonder her gallery Yeelen's emphasis on black experience and local culture has resulted in an art space in the service of something greater

In touch with her neighbourhood through her Jamaican roots as well as her living, breathing connection with its redevelopment, Karla gives us a unique view into Little Haiti. The working mom manages to find a Miami the whole family can enjoy—from transportative art to true Haitian flavour and kid-friendly adventures

How did your Miami story begin?

I first arrived in Miami from the Bronx, New York as a child in 1989. The city was different then—mostly a tourist destination. However, my family did not partake in much fun in the sun. We were new immigrants and saw the US as a place of opportunity where hard work and dedication could take you far. I noticed Miami was highly diverse. Every day I'd meet someone from a different country and soak up their differences. I decided I would love this place and I still do.

Your gallery was one of the first to regenerate Wynwood... Can you tell us why you moved to Little Haiti?

I opened *Yeelen* in Wynwood in 2006 in what felt like an industrial ghost town. Few people were around; it was a series of small streets with warehouses offering mechanical parts. There were few options for eating—maybe one little window to buy coffee. Once galleries set up shop, people were drawn in and the neighbourhood catapulted. But as so few people owned their spaces, developers bought up the area and displaced many to turn a profit. Little Haiti is different—it's larger, more accessible, and the commercial strips are dispersed throughout residential neighbourhoods. It's teeming with life thanks to mom-and-pop restaurants, bodegas and small businesses that draw people in.

What about the culture of the area?

Little Haiti is a quintessential Caribbean village: you can feel the tropical spirit all around. Vividly coloured buildings with handwritten signs, the smells of African-inspired foods, music playing in little shops... If you want fresh fruit there's always a street vendor cutting up sugar cane, roasting corn and splitting open coconuts full of fresh jelly.

Religious shops and "botanicas", like *Spirit & Beyond*, are found all over with fresh potted herbs hanging. I buy sage to burn in the gallery, uplifting the good vibes.

Where do you grab morning coffee?

I'm more of a tea person—I'm Jamaican! I like to go to *Buena Vista Deli* in the morning.

Are you worried Little Haiti will suffer Wynwood's fate?

Change is inevitable but if we want positive change we must preserve the heritage and identities that infused the magic in each neighbourhood. It's often the influence of the inhabitants that made those areas attractive in the first place.

Are there any local artists you're excited about?

I am excited about Miami-based artist Jerome Soimaud, whose studio is here in Little Haiti. His work is focussed on the everyday life of the people in African diaspora neighborhoods like Little Haiti, Liberty City, and Overtown. His large-scale canvasses with charcoal and graphite transport you to that particular space. In variations of grey you can feel colours, temperature and even movement. That's an impressive challenge when using what's essentially a pencil on a 60 × 60-square-inch (1.5 × 1.5 -square-metre) canvas. It takes real dedication to your subject.

What's the state of the art scene here?

Miami is a young art city much like my gallery is a young space. However, being young can be exciting and explorative; allowing one to take creative license and push limits. The only limits are those of our imaginations.

Are any of your peers in the art world doing anything interesting right now?

David Castillo has a great gallery out on the beach. Sadly, galleries usually hold openings on the same nights, leaving me little time to see what everyone else is up to.

Working aside, any favourite spots for romance and reconnection?

Miami is the Magic City, and there's definitely magic all around. It could be as simple as walking along the beach soaking up the moonlight or enjoying cuisine from restaurants from any particular country. Right now I'm loving— maybe a bit too much—Peruvian food. There is a great spot called *Sabor a Perú* close to the gallery— an absolute gem.

When you need some time away to recharge, where do you go?

I tend to go for a staycation and a favorite is *Soho Beach House.* You've got everything from sun, beach, food and drinks to program- ming that brings in live bands and DJs from all over the world. A weekend there can feel like a full-on vacation without the stress of flying.

Miami is known to many as a party city—so how does family life work?

I won't lie, Miami is a party city and that helps make it great. But for families there are definitely things to do. If you enjoy the water there is kayaking on the bay, chartering a boat, and other water-based activities—or parks such as *Oleta River State Park.* Culture-wise we have a pretty amazing new museum, the *PAMM*, where I just took in an inspiring show on Jean-Michel Basquiat. I haven't found many restaurants that aren't kid-friendly —as long as it's before 10pm. Also, go to the *Miami Children's Museum* if your kids are under ten, *Jungle Island, Fairchild Tropical Gardens*

and of course the beach. I usually go to Mid Beach.

How can visitors help areas like Little Haiti retain their identity as they become more popular?

Supporting local businesses and not big-box retail chains, so the dollars stay in the community.

Can you recommend some?

Chez Le Bebe. It might be a complete dive with terrible customer service, but the food is amazing! The "taso" (fried goat), is delicious. Another great restaurant is *Leela's*— you can sit down and take your time there. It's clean, healthy Haitian cuisine. Christine takes care of the place and she is awesome. As for shopping, *Libreri Mapou* is a bookstore with French, Haitian and African literature as well as books on spirituality. Mapou can get you everything, and he even gives Creole and history lessons. He's very knowledgeable—he's like one of our elders here. Next to the bookstore there's the *Little Haiti Thrift & Gift Store.* They update every few days so there's always something new to be found.

"Little Haiti" only recently became the official name. How do you like it?

I think it's great. For a while the battle was between calling it "Lemon City" or "Little Haiti" and my best response is I love lemons, but what is more dynamic than a cultural identity based on people… When you say Little Haiti I think of people, of the food, music, language and dance that draws from African and French culture primarily and just saying that makes me hungry. Great communities like Chinatown in New York or Little Italy are amazing because you get to experi- ence a country within another country—and that is magical.

Fighting the good fight to preserve biodiversity is the 83-acre Fairchild Tropical Botanic Garden, open since 1938

Mermaid of Miami

Gonzalo Torres Gimeno

Through the 1990s a cosy guesthouse at 909 Collins Avenue, Miami Beach hosted a procession of colourful characters. World-class musicians, incognito princesses and escaped inmates—the friendly Uruguayan proprietors welcomed them all. Here follow a few extracts from Gonzalo's diary...

August, 1992
Ana and I just arrived in Miami via Caracas. Hard to move country with one baby in tow and another on the way. It's been hotter than any heat we've ever known and we barely had more than a few dollars and a guitar to our name. Fortunately Papito's been here to sort us out. A guardian angel in a low-rider with hydraulic suspension and loud, loud speakers. He managed to come up with the papers we needed to buy a car. And the car. He was very taken with our little one, whom he calls "Princesita". I'm pretty sure he'll always be around to lend a helping hand.

July 1993
Somehow the two babies didn't wake up when we were busy ripping out the rotting carpets of this 40-year-old house. When we pulled up the first one a thick gleaming layer of maggots writhed at the sudden change in atmosphere. We will paint, saw, sand and hammer these ten rooms into a tiny Caribbean palace. 909 Collins Avenue—the Mermaid Guest House. Our children will grow up here.

March 1995
Today I caught my son running down the main corridor, a bunch of cameras hanging from his tiny shoulder. Trying to keep up behind him was the Japanese photographer from Room 8, worried to death about his precious equipment. Seems like he'd struck up a friendship with Gonzalo Jr. and was answering all his questions about how to take pictures, when the little one took advantage of a distraction to run off with the loot. Yoshi was shaking with relief when I gave them back to him, and he made a date to take a portrait of the boy—for a Japanese album cover.

December 1997
With the New Year on its way we can finally relax after a difficult year, thanks to a strange intervention. Just before Christmas we were sitting in the patio talking about how badly the season was going, when we were interrupted from above. The guest in the penthouse was leaning over the balcony—he'd heard everything. And amazingly, he offered to help us out by renting his suite from December to March and paying everything up front! Naturally, we agreed. Even to his strange condition of repainting the room. By the end of the week he was like another member of the family. Rosellor, our Haitian housekeeper with an enormous heart, told us he'd already repainted the room and even purchased a flat screen TV. But then, a few days later, he disappeared. No sign of him for days. When we finally gave up hope of seeing him again, we ventured up into the room to find it... painted completely black. I managed to get in touch with his sister, who told us he'd escaped from a mental health facility in New York a few days before arriving at the Mermaid. For us he'll always be another guardian angel, sent when we most needed him.

September 1998
Just got home from Papito's. His son Ricky turned one and they really
threw the house out the window. The kids had a fantastic time—they
loved little Ricky's pinstripe suit and gold chains—"just like daddy".
Another big hit was the piñata, filled with candy and dollar bills. What
a night it was, with everyone celebrating in the same living room.
They were so happy to receive our bottle of champagne that Papito
repaid us with the kind of green that made me realise he's not actually
a professional baseball player. To think I was so impressed by all
those official jerseys...

December 1999
Late last night, a beautiful Middle Eastern woman came into the hotel
with her labrador retriever. She was crying inconsolably, desperate
for a place to spend the night. She told us she'd just run away from her
violent husband. She had no documents, no money... But promised she'd
pay in full as soon as she can. We sat her down in the patio with a glass
of water. We explained that we didn't have any vacancies—everything
was booked and the penthouse hadn't been cleaned after a late checkout.
But when she broke down again, we decided to quickly clean up the
suite. A little while after she'd settled a bit, she went out to walk her
dog—only to come back even more distraught. It was the night before
New Year's Eve and the streets were filled with people. And she lost the

dog—her only friend in this world—in the chaos. It was three in the morning and I went out to look for him. I pushed through the packed streets until I finally came up against a note stuck on a post: a labrador retriever had been found.

January 2000
We just received a package. The letter inside had a letterhead reading "His Royal Highness". And the envelope was filled with enough cash to cover our mysterious guest's stay three times over—as well as a dress embroidered with gold thread. The letter was from her parents. They declared it a small token of appreciation for having helped their daughter —"the princess"—in her time of need.

April 2000
Our dear friend, the percussionist Carlitos Ventién came over to the bar to drown his sorrows again. Hard to believe he was once on stage in Woodstock, banging on his drums with Santana. But the happy memories aren't the ones that follow him around. One glass of wine sends him back to Vietnam. When our landlord came to argue about a change in the lease, he got into a rage and insulted Ana. Carlitos overheard and charged out to grab him by the neck. He lifted him clear off the ground, uttering things the children should not have heard. I feel like we might not be seeing him much around here any more.

July 2001
Today I turned the Kings into Gypsies. A mutual friend put me in touch with the band—so I went to pick them up from the Jackie Gleason Theater in our red Cadillac El Dorado with white leather seats. Amid the laughter I forgot there wasn't enough gasoline to get us back to the Mermaid, 15 blocks away. My shiny red collector's item sputtered to a stop, completely useless. Fresh from their sell-out show, the Gypsy Kings had to drag their luggage down the South Beach sidewalk in the oppressive heat. Surely this is the beginning of a lifelong friendship.

Today
Somehow 909 Collins Avenue remains empty, despite the hurricane of development that transformed everything around it. The sun has washed away the colours of the Mermaid Guest House but not the memories. They are still alive for the countless guests around the world who called it home—even just for one night.

Having lived in Ibiza and composed music for telenovelas in Caracas, Venezuela, singer-songwriter Gonzalo Torres Gimeno also once left his mark on an earlier incarnation of Miami Beach. He currently lives in Punta del Este, Uruguay with his wife Ana, making art in the forest and dreaming of a return to Miami

On the Pulse

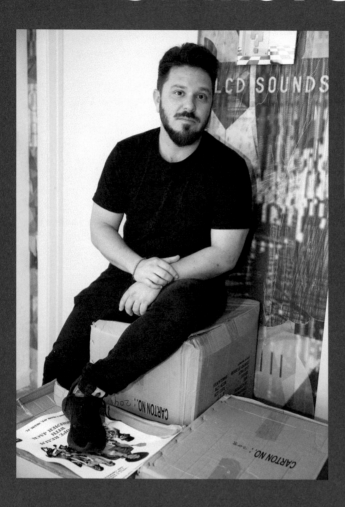

As the III Points Festival continues to turn the Miami music scene upside down, it's no surprise to discover that its organiser is also behind the ingenious programming of influential music spot Bardot. David started off running his own bars and clubs in Gainesville, Florida before coming to the Magic City to set it alight

Credited with bringing some musical freshness to a notoriously plastic city—David designs our perfect night out in Miami. Along the way he names local tunes to look out for, confesses his pizza passion—and helps us find our way off South Beach into the real soul of the city

Through your work with Bardot and III Points, you've aimed at creating authentic music spaces in a city known for its flash. How?

As a business person, any time you do a project, you're looking to fill a void, to offer something that doesn't exist creatively and conceptually. From rock to techno and hip hop to future beats, I love programming all types of music. I never do a show I don't believe in. I think it's a blessing that Miami doesn't have enough of that, because it allows me to do something natural and sincere in a market that needs it. Good projects need to be well-timed, thought-out and consistent. I've been at it for six years, and in Miami terms, that's not really normal for most projects.

What's your way to get lost in Miami?

By smoking some of that good stuff we have here... But seriously, walking around in Miami is hard. It's not like other cities. There are pockets and you have to drive— Uber and Lyft between them. Public transportation is just getting started. So it's actually hard to get lost because you always need your GPS.

Can you tell us a little about the neighbourhood where Bardot is? Are there any local spots you like for dinner before a show or a night out?

Bardot is on the hinge of the Design District and Wynwood, so it has a nice meld between this luxurious high-end area and a hipster grassroots vibe. It's in the artistic epicentre of Miami—it's highbrow meets lowbrow design, diverse clientele; the sound can vary depending on the night. We take our artists to *Mandolin Aegean Bistro*, which is a really good Middle Eastern-style restaurant, really fresh. *Gigi* is another favourite late night spot. It's open till 5am, so we can take them there after the gigs. I like

the soba and the buns there. It's got like a Momofuku kind of vibe. It reminds me of Transit in Berlin, this kind of fast, Asian-style service; it comes out quickly but with a nice vibe and energy to it.

Are there any local names you've been proud to see come up at Bardot? Or other artists you're excited about?

For sure, some of those names that have played Bardot and are now doing big things, like The Jacuzzi Boys, Psychic Mirrors, Danny Daze, Nick Leon. I think those are some of the people we've seen rising through the ranks, from playing small shows with us to being booked for the festival. Right now The Guest Poets are great, they're a two piece rock and roll band. Mister Brown is an avid record collector. He's the best vinyl, keeping-it-real DJ— he opened for Floating Points for us, opened up for James Murphy. We can really put him anywhere.

Tell us about the state of nightlife in Miami today. What effect have festivals like Ultra and WMC had?

When I got here in 2010 there was a lot of dance music in North America. These markets were getting the boom and upside of EDM and became committed to it. Here, this kind of music is still prominent and there are still lots of people making money off of it, but I think we're seeing the tail end right now. For every cool person in Miami there's five douchebags— they don't even have to live here, they could be from the douchebag capitals of the world, and there's a lot of money in that douchebag culture. But there's been this really cool scene that I can't even describe as up-and-coming any more. It's begun to establish itself now and there's people outside my own group that have been working hard towards creating something. From Diego and Will at *Electric Pickle* to Davide and Paloma at *Trade*, Rebecca and DJ Tennis Manfredi doing The Plot and pop-up parties; the guys behind *Treehouse*, us at Bardot, even *Churchill's Pub* with the punk scene. You get an overload on one side of the spectrum and a complete riot against it on the other. The misidentification of Miami gave us all a little chip on our shoulders to do more and balance out the equation. I think that's happened over the past six years—it's been a transformation because of the call and response of North American EDM music. Many festivals pertain to that and I think it's a dying trend. Tons of international labels have been pulling out because they've noticed the decline.

Sometimes we need comfort food—any go-to places to cure a hangover?
I love pizza—and though Miami's not known for its pizza there's still a couple I love. Like *EastSide Pizza*. *Steve's Pizza* is the best. Then you've got hangover brunch—especially places like *Blue Collar*, their breakfast is dope. Miami has a lot of great Peruvian food, like *Sabor a Perú* in what developers now like to call Edgewater.

OK, we're on a long-haul party adventure—what's the itinerary?
A good place to start off is Bardot, then off to Trade on a Friday to see Link Miami Rebels. Then you need to decompress and the perfect way to do that is with one of the island parties the guys from Treehouse organise—they ship you out to an island off the coast of Miami to party for the day. After that you come back, shower and get decent before heading out to The Electric Pickle and then end up at *Club Space*. You have to end up at Space but you have to be very careful who plays or you could find yourself in a very different scene.

What is the greatest Miami misconception?
I think it's like anything else these days, people glance over things and make assumptions really quickly. This social media, clickbait, headline-only culture... For people who've just been once or had a friend who went or who've seen something from afar, it's easy to assume Miami is Vegas by the sea. It's like any city—until you actually spend some time here you can't know what's good. You don't have to dig too far, but you have to do your research and go to the right spots. Once here you can truly experience the diversity of the city, the people, the fact that it's super young. It's still the Wild West of North America. It's not buttoned-up corporate New York, not scenester, close-at-2am, selfie-taking Los Angeles. It's a party atmosphere with lots of cultures converging in one space and people who do give a shit about music. The places where they choose to consume it are fresh, innovative spaces.

The lead-up to your festival must be an exciting, stressful time—where do you like to go to unwind?
The Standard Spa is definitely my go-to. It's at a very interesting longitude and latitude in Miami. It's a magical spot committed to wellness and relaxation. There's also a beautiful pool area and hammam. You can spend the day there and get centred really quickly.

What would the perfect Miami soundtrack consist of?
Uncle Loop, some booty bass from 2LiveCrew, Danny Daze—some of the stuff he's been putting out off Omnidisc. Definitely Psychic Mirrors—they have an incredible, funky, synth-driven sound that blends these genres together. And then there's so much good hip hop and future beats—Denzel Curry,

Local boy Daniel Serfer gave up criminal law to become a restaurateur—taste the reason why at his diner Blue Collar

Sweat Records
Little Haiti

Radio-Active Records
Fort Lauderdale

Nick Leon, Rob Banks, coming up on the hip hop side. If you want to know what's good from the 18 year olds making music here, know that the hip hop movement is super good. Tripped out but hardcore hip hop MCs—the beats are no joke.

Any interesting record shops for the travelling cratedigger?
    Sweat Records definitely. And if you're feeling more adventurous for the hike out to Fort Lauderdale, *Radio-Active Records*.

Is there something you wish visitors knew?
    That's a tough one. I think a lot of people, when they come, they want to stay on the water. They go to the beach, obviously. If you end up on South Beach, you end up missing some of the best parts of Miami and the local scene. What I'd

want them to know is that even if you're staying on the water, be prepared to spend a lot of time on the mainland. Otherwise you might think South Beach is Miami—and that would be a misrepresentation.

Shuttered Speed

A showcase by Ivan Santiago

The Miami native's work has adorned the city's most prestigious spaces. This extract from his series "TwentyFour-Seven" depicts urban lanscapes that exist as a by-product of Miami's constant consumption

Antonia Wright, Artist

Personal Spaces

The bank of the Miami River provides a starting point for Antonia's journey through the city—showing off the most inspiring spot for artistic wine-drinking and boat-watching, sharing which gallery has the best third floor, and explaining what sandwich to eat at midnight

How does the city inspire you?

Anything by the water in Miami inspires me. I love running over the Key Biscayne Bridge. You see water on all sides and a beautiful view of the city. If you go early evening midweek you can often be the only person on the beach— so you feel like it's your own private island. I also love running on the boardwalk on Miami Beach. It starts at The Bass museum and goes north for about two miles. My studio is on the Miami River and I love taking our little boat up and down. One place for some inspiring history is the *Freedom Tower*. This is the Cuban Ellis Island. All the Cubans came through this beautiful building in the 1960s.

What does your typical Miami day look like?

I live and work in Little Havana/ Miami River so my activities centre around there. I also go to Wynwood/ Design District and Little Haiti. I have a baby son so I wake up pretty early. I go to *Skanda Yoga* at 9:30am—the best studio in Miami. Then I shower and get to work. My studio is right on the river and it's very inspiring—I see manatees and dolphins swimming by and now we have a little turtle that lives by our seawall. I work in the studio most days and walk my dog afternoons by Jose Marti Park.

Where would you go for lunch or coffee?

Oriental Bakery & Grocery is a great low-key lunch spot down the street. It's run by a Palestinian family and the babaghanoush is amazing. For lunch, *Buena Vista Deli*, or *Lemoni Café* are great. I love vegetarian and vegan food and *The Honey Tree* and *The Last Carrot* are delicious. *Panther Coffee* in Wynwood has great cold-brew ice coffee, or try any Cuban "ventanita" or coffee window for strong, sugary espresso.

What about for a typical dinner?

I often walk over the Flagler Bridge and go to *Soya e Pomodoro* —a great Italian restaurant with outside seating and live music. Anything with eggplant there is amazing, and all the pasta is good. They're all Italians and it has a really good vibe. *Niu Kitchen* is also delicious. They do Spanish tapas, but it's innovative. The cold tomato soup is delicious. For a drink, *The Corner* has a good happy hour.

Art Basel made Miami the focus of the art world. Is that a blessing or a curse?

A huge blessing. Sure there are criticisms of Art Basel getting out of hand and people coming for parties rather than art, but Miami's art boom over the last two decades is largely a result of the fair coming to town. I think it helps everyone in the art community if they have a deadline to finish projects every year.

Which galleries shouldn't we miss?

Spinello Projects! Although I am a little biased—they represent me. Currently I have an exhibition at *Locust Projects* with 90 night-blooming jasmine plants. But they always have a really good programme. Then, *The Screening Room* is an experimental video art gallery in Wynwood. *Noguchi Breton*, formerly GucciVuitton, is another alternative space run by artists. And for museums—the *ICA*, *The Bass*... But if you had three days in Miami I'd go to the new one, *PAMM*. It's a big, beautiful museum, right on the water. You can sit outside and watch boats and drink wine. *The Margulies Collection* is not to be missed as well. It's one of the world's largest photo collections. Now they have the

Not-for-profit space Locust Projects is all about allowing artists to experiment outside the usual industry pressures

biggest Anselm Kiefer show that's ever been held in the US.

What specific artworks do you keep going back to?
   Ana Mendieta's work in the *de la Cruz Collection*, third floor. She was an incredible Cuban artist. On the same floor, Félix González-Torres. Plus, the Margulies has a very rare sculpture from Willem de Kooning. It's one of my favourite things.

And where can we see fresh local art?
   The *National YoungArts Foundation* campus showcases the work of younger people from all over the country. In front they have a gallery and the back space they call the Old Bacardi Building—it's like a box made of stained glass. They're developing workspaces there for young artists—they offer a prize and all students can apply.

You are also a poet. Any good reads for Miami you'd recommend?
   Exile Books is a local press and Daniel Feinberg, a local poet, just published a book of poems titled "Bora Bora Bora". My mom, the writer Carolina Garcia-Aguilera, has published the "Lupe Solano" mystery series, all set in Miami. Three bodies per book or you get your money back. I am a little biased, but I think they are the best.

What's the perfect soundtrack for the city?
   Anything by the Jacuzzi Boys. They're a local band—friends of mine. They have a beachy-punky kind of feel. They play a lot at *Churchill's* in Little Haiti. They just opened for Iggy Pop. A good venue for bands is the *Jackie Gleason Theater*. They used to do old shows there—it's a beautiful old theatre.

It might look like a gas station, but Chef Creole offers Miami's whole cultural melting pot in one delicious kitchen

But now they do a lot of concerts. My partner, Ruben Millares, is in a new band, Chicken Liquor. We just made a music video together.

Where else for some tunes?
Ball and Chain is a bar-club with live music in Little Havana on Calle Ocho. It was an old bar from the 1920s—they have pictures of the Rat Pack there—but the new owners revitalised it. They have a stage outside built in the shape of a coconut. Another one is *Hoy Como Ayer*, it's been around forever and has great Cuban music. For dancing I go to *Rec Room* on Miami Beach.

You're of Cuban decent. How do we get on that Cuban vibe in Miami?
El Palacio de Los Jugos hands down. It's another country. They sell fruits and vegetables, there's a guy who cuts coconut and they have

huge slabs of dried fish hanging from the ceiling. First time I went I turned around too fast and got smacked in the face by a huge dried cod. *La Carreta* is good standard Cuban food, there's a bunch of them in Miami. I always get "camarones al ajillo" (shrimp in garlic sauce), or any of the "platanos maduros" or "tostones", beans and rice... In Wynwood a lot of people go to *Enriqueta's Sandwich Shop*—a really low-down Cuban diner. They do a sandwich called the "medianoche", because you're supposed to eat it at midnight. It's got every type of pork and ham you could think of with cheese, bright yellow mustard and pickles on this sweet bread. *El Mago de las Fritas* is another one. The "frita" is a Cuban sandwich, like a hamburger made with sausage patty, and with shoestring French fries on it. I don't really eat that

Paradise island: The Standard Spa Miami Beach will give birth to a new you on its own little landmass

kind of food but my boyfriend would eat there every day.

But though everyone talks about Cuban, there's so many other foods right now. I live in a Honduran neighbourhood—they have these "baleadas" (tortillas with mashed fried beans) that are everywhere now. Then there's Haitian food, Bahamian... I just had friends in town from New York and we went to *Chef Creole* in Little Haiti. It's amazing! It's a take-out place but you can also sit at the side and somebody will take your order. My friends wanted to eat there every day. They have tons of fried seafood, homemade sauces, and "peas and rice".

When you finish a big project, where would you celebrate?

Michael's Genuine makes really really good food—all locally sourced. Then *Joe's Stone Crab* is a staple in Miami. When the crabs are in season they're absolutely delicious. They have a restaurant, but I prefer to take out and picnic on the beach. It's indulgent—expensive but really good. I recently went to *Beaker & Gray* after installing at Locust Projects, sat at the bar, and had some really good drinks and food. When I'm working on a show I work really late and they serve till 2/3am. They have a special after 11pm with cheaper drinks and foods. I always get the mushroom plate and the octopus.

And where do you go to relax?

After Basel finishes every year, I treat myself to a day at *The Standard Spa* on Miami Beach. The steam room heals.

Shifting Sands

A litter of close-knit, creative locals have been turning the sunny isle into a more refined destination. From a burgeoning cocktail scene to world-class art venues, Miami's South Beach is growing up

Culture | **New World Order**

Put your shirt back on—there's high culture to be found in this former swamp. At the crossroads between music and architecture, the *New World Center* is leading Miami Beach's cultural renaissance. The state-of-the-art structure was created by architect Frank Gehry—as his first Miami oeuvre—in tandem with conductor Michael Tilson Thomas. It's home campus to the New World Symphony—an academy designed to prepare the globe's next crop of top orchestral musicians. But it's not all high brow. The varied programme includes late-night shows featuring DJs and breathtaking visuals. The lush "Soundscape" garden hosts free movie screenings and public yoga. And the insanely vast projection wall provides free stimulation to picnickers—shirtless or not.
• New World Center, 500 17th Street, South Beach, nws.edu

The Classics

Back in 1913, Joe's was the only lunch counter on the Beach. But after he discovered a local species of edible crab, his haunt became favoured by the likes of Al Capone. *Joe's Stone Crab* still serves it the same, with butter, lemon and a side of coleslaw; and rivalled only by the key lime pie. Go at lunch to beat the dinner crowds. Meanwhile, at *Puerto Sagua*, it's heresy to try just one dish. The avocado salad with red onion is perfection, black beans and rice are a staple—but don't miss the shredded beef heaven, or "ropa vieja" ("dirty laundry"). If you're on the go, grab a Cuban coffee and a "midnight" sandwich off the hot plate.
• South Beach, various locations, see Index p. 64

Food **Clean and Dirty**

Healthy and sustainable food might be one thing, but culinary joy must be at the centre of the experience. That's the view at least of Chef Nicole Votano. Ergo, *Dirt* might offer vegetarian, vegan, gluten-free for breakfast, lunch or dinner. But you can also get a solid steak sandwich with farm-to-table ingredients. The interior echoes the dietary vibe with a clean, fresh, almost Nordic look. Try creative, reasonably priced creations like lavender lattes with almond milk, acai bowls or the simple but perfect avocado bread.
• Dirt, 232 5th Street, South Beach, dirteatclean.com

Night **Deuce in the Hole**

Sadly, you can't meet Mac Klein no more. The local legend bought his bar the year JFK was killed, and wore his signature Hawaiian shirt to work every day until 2016, when he passed away at age 101. His legacy—at first sight a plain dive bar with checkered floors, pool table and jukebox—is the oldest remaining watering hole in the city. It's one of those rare spots where a total stranger can feel like a best friend—like the Miami version of "Cheers". Mac Klein himself always said that if everybody could meet at *Club Deuce*, there'd be no war...
• Mac's Club Deuce, 222 14th Street, South Beach, macsclubdeuce.com

Turning Tricks

Spend a few minutes in *South Pointe Park* (pictured) and you'll notice most people are on wheels. They're not just getting from point A to point B though—but showing off some flair as they dart around some DIY obstacle courses. It won't be long before you're convinced of your own hidden ability to pop 180s and cruise quarter pipes—or at the very least take miniature glides while gripping onto the closest railing. So head over to *Fritz's* and get a pair of rental blades. Join the locals, learn some tricks, and perhaps remember what a skinned knee feels like all over again.
• South Beach, various locations, see Index p. 64

Food **Stand Up, Chow Down**

For a snappy lunch en route to the golden sands and lapping waves, there's two local street food stars. Though *My Ceviche*—started by a Mexican-Colombian duo—has spots across the city, the original location might be where to try the marinated seafood dish. At a pinch, look out for stone crab claws, too. Meanwhile, blue tacos are the looker at *Taquiza* (pictured), made with ethical corn from Mexico. This tasteful place keeps it simple with its taco selection and a few other more elaborate options like Mexican eggs.
• My Ceviche, 1250 S Miami Ave, myceviche.com; Taquiza, 1506 Collins Ave, taquizamiami.com

Night **Rainbow Flagship**

When Gianni Versace moved to South Beach in 1992 he became a trailblazer for a queer revolution in an area scarred by drug wars. And it's still a Disneyland for the LGBT community—with venues suiting every persuasion. The longest running is *Palace*, famous for drag shows including Sunday's "Brunchic". Don't be shy—straight people enjoy the burgers too. *Twist* offers three dancefloors, world-class DJs and a raunchy crowd on any night. But if it seems a little white-centric, try *Club Boi*. Touted as a gay club for brothers and those who love them, its eclectic parties keep the friendly vibes flowing.
• South Beach, various locations, see Index p. 64

Decked Out

If you make it to Miami before Spring 2017, you'll find art museum *The Bass* closed for transformation. But that won't stop you appreciating the iconic Art Deco architecture of the former public library, bought in 1964 to house the collection of Austrian-Jewish immigrants John Bass and Johanna Redlich. On its façade is a neon art installation by Sylvie Fleury that reads "Eternity Now". Ponder this metaphysical conundrum until the Beach's principal art space reopens, with 50% more exhibition space and shiny new educational facilities too. Or simply take a walk around the neighbourhood to gaze on more examples of the architectural trend that symbolised Miami Beach's boom years of the 1930s. The street on which the Bass stands is named after John Collins, who along with Carl Fisher was responsible for turning a mangrove swamp into a stunning holiday resort and magnet for the millionaire crowd. The area between South Beach's 6th and 23rd Streets is officially designated as the Art Deco District, making it the perfect place to view Miami's adaptation of the aesthetic trend that originated in Paris. Known as "Tropical Deco", the Florida take involves floral licks, nautical themes, and, of course, plenty of heartwarming pastel colours.
• The Bass, 2100 Collins Avenue, South Beach, thebass.org

Glass Half Full

When Gabriel Orta and his partner Elad Zvi opened up a temporary cocktail pop-up in 2012, they had little idea of the wave they'd make in the coastal city. Pretty soon they had a permanent home at the Freehand Hotel, followed by offshoots in Chicago and LA. While consulting on cocktails worldwide, they also keep the juices of a new collaborative bar culture flowing back home

Miami is one of the few cities in the world best narrated while looking through a cocktail glass. Taking us through a place he describes as one big holiday is Gabriel Orta, who tips us off on late-night coffee windows, delicious egg-yolk dishes and where a lucky surfer might get to play with dolphins

What was your original home, and what's your home now?

I came over from Colombia in 1992, at 16 years old. Ever since, the beach has been my home. These days I live in Miami Beach. There are a lot of tourists, but also many locals. So it's kind of like being on a permanent vacation—with your friends around.

When you started Broken Shaker, did you envision the impact it would have on Miami?

Living here for so many years we knew Miami was ready for a change, and that locals and our friends would embrace it. We also knew from the get-go we had a good concept and a good chance of succeeding. We just just didn't expect it to take off so quickly. I guess the first time we were nominated for the James Beard Award—back then we didn't even own a bar, we were just a pop-up— we started to realise what was possible for us.

Which cocktail was Miami pre-Broken Shaker, and which is it now?

Before it was the Apple Martini. Now it's the Old Fashioned.

Take us on a tour through the city's cocktail scene.

One of the best places is *Sweet Liberty*. It's only been open six months and it's kind of the industry hangout for the bar and restaurant scene. It has a great atmosphere and great hospitality. You definitely need to have their frozen banana daiquiri, in a huge glass. Then, check out *The Anderson*, a 1980s-inspired place in an upcoming neighbourhood. My favourite drink there is the "I am too old for this shit". They also have a tiki bar in the back; always nice and affordable. Another place is *The Regent Cocktail Club*. It was the first classy cocktail bar in Miami. They always have piano music or Sinatra playing. They only have like five cocktails, but they change the menu often. A truly beautiful place for a date, or to relax and talk. Finally, *Repour Bar*—Isaac Grillo is always behind the bar. Always go for the bartender's choice.

You guys are cocktail trailblazers in Miami—is there an equivalent for dining?

I have to mention *Michael's Genuine Food & Drink*. Michael is the godfather of the Miami restaurant scene. When he opened in 2007, he was the first one to really focus on local ingredients and quality produce. Before him, Miami restaurants basically had one and the same menu. He's truly an inspiration for all Miami's chefs and bartenders —he took it to the next level.

Does that mean the produce scene has improved as well?

Yes—the *Coconut Grove Organic Market* is a good place to source for ingredients. Also try *Robert Is Here* in Homestead for local ingredients and proper sausages. Then, *Zak The Baker* for all your bread needs.

Any good food trucks or small eateries you like?

Catch Della Bowls food truck at *The Wynwood Yard* for the healthy option, or *Myumi* food truck for a omakase sushi experience like no other.

Out of a gazillion expensive restaurants in the city, which are actually worth the money?

Alter in Wynwood is worth every penny. The menu is always changing, but, there's usually a delicious vegan dish with leeks. And an egg-yolk dish that's incredible. *Naoe* in Brickell has amazing Japanese food. Go for the chef's menu, the omakase sushi—and don't miss out on the amazing sake, produced by the chef's family back in Japan

The Anderson drips with 1980s style and offers a drink called "I'm too old for this shit"... Which you might be

MIA Skate Shop
South Beach

Bardot
Wynwood

Electric Pickle
Wynwood

El Rey de las Fritas
Little Havanna

Taquiza
South Beach

Panther Coffee
South Beach

All Day
Downtown

*You're a skater as well as a shaker...
How's the scene?*

Skateboarding is like restaurants in Miami—it's very up-and-coming and there's not that many places. The guys from *MIA Skate Shop* just built a little skate park under a little bridge in Downtown. It's my favourite place to forget the world and just skate some ramps. It's good for the community.

Are there any clubs you'd recommend?

Bardot and *Electric Pickle* never disappoint.

Miami is a melting pot for people from Cuba down through South America. Any tips to experience the vibes?

I always like to go to the Cuban cafeterias. You have empanadas, a little window to get coffee late—it's a slice of Cuban culture. Another place in Little Havana is *El Rey de*

las Fritas, where you get this amazing Cuban burger with crispy potatoes and fried meat—it's really good. *Taquiza* is a taco spot on the beach. Their homemade blue corn tortillas are amazing, you don't want to miss them for lunch or late night. It's always a hit. The "lengua" (tongue) taco is very good, they braise the meat for a long time. Or the "nopales" (cactus) taco, is also amazing.

What about for some serious coffee?

There is this guy at *Panther Coffee* who came from Portland and brought this Stumptown Coffee vibe. He goes to Colombia, Brazil, gets all these single village coffees and roasts them himself. Very special. There's another place called *All Day*, downtown. The lady there is really good with different types of coffee.

58

Playing a lead role in the Miami music scene's resurgence—and Wynwood's transformation—is bar-venue Electric Pickle

Which Miami vice should be avoided?
Drinking frozen daiquiris with a upside-down corona in them.

Where would you go on a getaway?
One place I love is Eleuthera Island, right off the main Bahama island to the northeast. Surfer's Beach there is beautiful, there's a lot of locals and a killer little restaurant with amazing corn salad and corn fritters. Don't miss that. Once I went in a friend's boat so we could surf all weekend. It was like a perfect scene. We got into the water at 6am when the sun was just coming up and all of a sudden—we thought we were surrounded by sharks. But then we realised we were surrounded by a family of dolphins, like 12 of them. They played with us for 20 minutes while we surfed. It was incredible!

Miami is sometimes seen as a hedonistic Disneyland. What's your view?
Miami used to get a bad rap because it was a transient city full of tourists and cheesy things to do. But now it's done a 180-degree turn. It's always been a beautiful city surrounded by water, but what's making it special now is the sense of community. Now, chefs can open their own little restaurants, bartenders have their own bars. Artists have different galleries to showcase their work. It's becoming a great community and a place where families want to live. That's what's making it special.

Chucherías

ORISHA YEMAYA

Burning Siren

Yemayá is queen of the seas and mother of all deities in Yoruba—a religion that originated in West Africa and came to Miami mostly via Cuba. She's a good one to have on your side—bring Yemayá home for support in the realms of love, creativity or, at the very least, home décor.
• Yemayá, Botánica Negra Francisca, Little Havana

Books

Bad Monkey
• Carl Hiaasen, 2013

A regular columnist for the "Miami Herald", Hiaasen is known to take inspiration from news stories in his novels. In this characteristically mischievous comic thriller, a cop has an arm in his freezer and hopes to use it to get a promotion. He picks up an array of freaky characters while slaloming from Miami via Florida Keys to the Bahamas.

Rum Punch
• Elmore Leonard, 1992

Tarantino knew Leonard as a modern master of tight, sparse crime fiction. Which is why he adapted this tale of smuggling stewardess Jackie Brown, who gets caught by the police and placed in an impossible dilemma. The prolific author had sold tens of millions of copies of his novels by the time of his death in 2013.

Miami
• Joan Didion, 1987

"Havana vanities come to dust in Miami." So begins this thrilling non-fiction book that made waves at the time of its publication. From Castro to Ortega and the Bay of Pigs to Watergate, Didion dives with relish into the murky agendas that have affected Miami's Cuban communities.

Films

Any Given Sunday
• Oliver Stone, 1999

This tale of fictional football team Miami Sharks is so rich on great scenes, beautiful shots and memorable dialogue it's almost sad to compare it with Stone's subsequent work. Al Pacino's locker room talk is one of cinema's great speeches.

There's Something About Mary
• Farrelly Bros, 1998

Indulge in the frivolous, pastel-coloured side of Miami Beach with this dumbass comedy filled with memorably cringeworthy moments and an on-set soundtrack from Jonathan Richman.

Caddyshack
• Harold Ramis, 1980

This cult comedy takes on the Florida golfing scene with aplomb, featuring a young Bill Murray as a lunatic groundsman waging war on the gopher population.

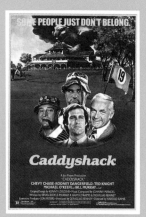

Music

Hold On I'm Comin'
• Sam & Dave, 1966

At a low-key Miami nightclub in 1961, two young singers met. Sam Moore and Dave Prater would go on to be the most successful soul duo ever, bringing gospel sounds to the hit parade. Though this seminal LP was recorded at Stax Records, Tennessee, the spark surely came from those warm Miami nights.

The Bass That Ate Miami
• Various Artists, 1988

"The bass that ate Miami must have partied really hard", promises the title track off this compilation. Mostly featuring work by genre granddaddy James McCauley under his various aliases, the record is a crash course in the bombastic, electro-leaning sound known as Miami Bass.

KC and the Sunshine Band
• KC and the Sunshine Band, 1975

The Miami disco funksters pumped out plenty of megahits... "Get Down Tonight" features on this, their second studio album, along with other, only-in-the-1970s creations like "Boogie Shoes"—sure to put a spring in your step as you strut down to the beach.

LOST iN

The City

Getting lost in the city is not about throwing away the map
It's about surrendering yourself to the essence of the place
The art and creativity that provide its individual inspiration
The sights, smells, flavours and sounds that make it unique

Also available from LOST iN

Next Issue: TOKYO

LOSTIN.COM

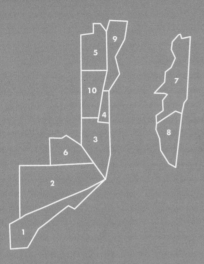

Districts

1. Coconut Grove
2. Coral Way
3. Downtown
4. Edgewater
5. Little Haiti
6. Little Havana
7. Mid Beach
8. South Beach
9. Upper East Side
10. Wynwood

Ⓒ Culture
Ⓕ Food
Ⓝ Night
Ⓞ Outdoors
Ⓢ Shop

1/ Coconut Grove

Coconut Grove Organic Market
3300 Grand Avenue
glaserorganicfarms.com
→ p. 57 Ⓢ

The Last Carrot
3133 Grand Avenue
+1 305 445 0805
lastcarrot.com
→ p. 48 Ⓕ

Vizcaya Museum & Gardens
3251 South Miami Avenue
vizcaya.org
→ p. 11 Ⓞ

2/ Coral Way

Hoy Como Ayer
2212 SW 8th Street
hoycomoayer.us
→ p. 16, 50 Ⓝ

Monserrate
2093 Coral Way
mimonserrate.com
→ p. 15 Ⓕ

Oriental Bakery & Grocery
1760 SW 3rd Ave
orientalbakerygrocery.com → p. 48 Ⓢ

Skanda Yoga
1800 SW
1st Avenue #102
skandayoga.com
→ p. 48 Ⓞ

3/ Downtown

All Day
1035 North Miami Avenue
alldaymia.com
→ p. 58 Ⓕ

Club Space
34 NE
11th Street
clubspace.com
→ p. 32 Ⓝ

El Tucán
1111 SW 1st Avenue
eltucanmiami.com
→ p. 16 Ⓕ

Freedom Tower
600 Biscayne Blvd
mdcmoad.org
→ p. 48 Ⓞ

Jungle Island
1111 Parrot Jungle Trail
jungleisland.com
→ p. 24 Ⓞ

Miami Children's Museum
980 MacArthur Causeway
miamichildrens museum.org
→ p. 24 Ⓒ

Miami Marine Stadium
3501 Rickenbacker Causeway
+1 305 361 3316
→ p.6 Ⓞ

Naoe
661 Brickell Key Drive
naoemiami.com
→ p. 57 Ⓕ

Niu Kitchen
134 NE
2nd Avenue
niukitchen.com
→ p. 48 Ⓕ

Pérez Art Museum Miami (PAMM)
1103 Biscayne Boulevard
pamm.org
→ p. 10, 24, 48 Ⓒ

Soya e Pomodoro
120 NE 1st Street
soyaepomodoro.com
→ p. 48 Ⓕ

The Corner
1035 North Miami Avenue
thecornermiami.com
→ p. 48 Ⓝ

4/ Edgewater

Enriqueta's Sandwich Shop
186 NE 29th Street
→ p. 50 Ⓕ

Mignonette
210 NE 18th Street
mignonettemiami.com
→ p. 8 Ⓕ

National YoungArts Foundation
2100 Biscayne Boulevard
youngarts.org
→ p. 49 Ⓒ

Sabor A Perú
2923 Biscayne Boulevard
saboraperu.net
→ p. 24, 32 Ⓕ

5/ Little Haiti

3x3 Santa Barbara Botanica
5700 NE 2nd Avenue
→ p. 18 Ⓢ

Buena Vista Deli
4590 NE 2nd Avenue
buenavistadeli.com
→ p. 15, 23, 48 Ⓕ

Chef Creole
200 NW 54th Street
chefcreole.com
→ p. 21, 50 Ⓕ

Chez Le Bebe
114 NE 54th Street
chezlebebe.com
→ p. 24 Ⓕ

Churchill's Pub
5501 NE 2nd Avenue
churchillspub.com
→ p. 20, 32, 49 Ⓝ

Clive's Cafe
5890 NW 2nd Avenue
clivescafe.com
→ p. 20 Ⓕ

de la Cruz Collection
23 NE 41st Street
delacruzcollection.org
→ p. 49 Ⓒ

Fifi Records
159 NE 54th Street #1
→ p. 19 Ⓢ

Fiorito
5555 NE 2nd Avenue
fioritomiami.com
→ p. 15 Ⓕ

Institute of Contemporary Art
4040 NE 2nd Avenue
icamiami.org
→ p. 48 Ⓒ

Ironside Pizza
7580 NE 4th Court
pizzaironside.com
→ p. 19 Ⓕ

The Standard Spa
40 Island Avenue
Beach
standardhotels.com
→ p. 32, 51 Ⓞ

The Regent
Cocktail Club
1690 Collins Avenue
Beach
ldvhospitality.com
→ p. 57 Ⓝ

The Webster
1220 Collins Avenue
Beach
thewebster.us
→ p. 9 Ⓢ

Trade
1439 Washington
Avenue Beach
trademia.com
→ p. 32 Ⓝ

Twist
1057 Washington
Avenue Beach
twistsobe.com
→ p. 54 Ⓝ

9/ Upper East Side

Beacon Hill Chocolates
6318 Biscayne
Boulevard #100
beaconhillchocolates.
com → p. 15 Ⓢ

Blue Collar
6730 Biscayne
Boulevard
bluecollarmiami.com
→ p. 32 Ⓕ

EastSide Pizza
731 NE 79th Street
miamieastsidepizza.
com → p. 32 Ⓕ

Fly Boutique
7235 Biscayne
Boulevard
flyboutiquevintage.
com → p. 9 Ⓢ

The Anderson
709 NE 79th Street
theandersonmiami.
com → p. 57 Ⓝ

The Honey Tree
5138 Biscayne
Boulevard
+1 305 759 1696
→ p. 48 Ⓕ

10/ Wynwood

Alter Restaurant
223 NW 23rd Street
altermiami.com
→ p. 57 Ⓕ

Bardot
3456 North Miami
Avenue
bardotmiami.com
→ p. 31, 32, 58 Ⓝ

Beaker & Gray
2637 North Miami
Avenue
beakerandgray.com
→ p. 51 Ⓕ

Electric Pickle
2826 North Miami
Avenue
electricpicklemiami.
com → p. 31, 32, 58 Ⓝ

Gigi
3470 North Miami
Avenue
+1 305 573 1520
giginow
→ p. 31 Ⓕ

Myumi
160 NW 26th Street
myumifoods.com
→ p. 57 Ⓕ

Salumeria 104
3451 NE
1st Avenue #104
salumeria104.com
→ p. 14 Ⓕ

Style Mafia
2324 NW 5 Avenue
shopstylemafia.com
→ p. 9 Ⓢ

The Margulies
Collection
591 NW 27th Street
margulieswarehouse.
com → p. 48 Ⓒ

The Screening Room
2626 NW 2nd Avenue
thescreenin
groommiami.com
→ p. 48 Ⓒ

The Wynwood Yard
56 NW 29th Street
thewynwoodyard.com
→ p. 57 Ⓕ

Zak the Baker
405 NW 26th Street
zakthebaker.com
→ p. 57 Ⓢ

Other

Fairchild Tropical
Botanic Garden
Old Cutler Road, Coral
Gables, South Miami
fairchildgarden.org
→ p. 24 Ⓞ

El Mago De Las Fritas
5828 SW 8th Street,
West Miami
elmagodelasfritas.com
→ p. 50 Ⓕ

Steve's Pizza
12101 Biscayne
Boulevard,
North Miami
→ p. 32 Ⓕ

Radio-Active Records
845 North Federal
Highway,
Fort Lauderdale
radio-active-records.
com → p. 33 Ⓢ

Robert Is Here
19200 SW 344th
Street, Homestead
robertishere.com
→ p. 57 Ⓢ

ROSELINE

GEOFFREY PHILP

Story

Roseline

Geoffrey Philp

If Jesus Christ hadn't saved her from this, Roseline thought as she squeezed limes over the red snapper, why should she cling to Him? She had sacrificed everything for Him, but He had not clung to her. In fact, it seemed as if He was punishing her for leaving her father's house and marrying the man she loved. Her father's words were almost prophetic.

"This will not end well. Bad enough you had a child with that so-called Christian and left school. But if you leave here with him to worship his albino god, you are dead to me."

Roseline could understand her father's rage. Although Alcide had sent Roseline to the best private schools, he never stopped preparing her to become a mambo: teaching her all he knew about natural medicines and remedies. It was something Roseline had hoped to use when she became a medical doctor, to remove the stigma that her father had worked petwo—the dark side of vodou.

Whether the desire was out of guilt, love, or both, Roseline would never know. For when her boyfriend, Frantz, got on one knee, gave her a wedding ring, and asked her to move with him to Port-au-Prince, where they would raise their child, Stephanie, in a good Christian home--what else could she do? Perhaps, in the capital, she could even resume her studies.

Roseline moved to Port-au-Prince and brought the same devotion she had for the loas to the Friends of Jesus. For wasn't Jesus, about whom the nuns had taught her, the same as Lenglensou? Just as the Virgin Mary was Erzulie Freda?

Then, the earthquake changed everything. One minute Roseline and Stephanie were walking to the store and the next, Roseline was pulling Frantz's lifeless body from the rubble.

After a year of hardships, Roseline saved enough money to escape on a boat to Miami and went immediately to the headquarters of the Friends of Jesus for help. One of the elders, Roger Stephenson, took a special interest in her and Stephanie. Roger went as far as hiring Roseline as a janitor at the supermarket where he worked as the manager.

"Stephanie, you're going to be late," Roseline called out and put the fish beside a bowl of white rice.

"I can't believe you made pwason fris for him, maman. Even after what he did to me."

"The Bible says, 'Vengeance is mine,'" Roseline said and kissed Stephanie on her forehead. "Don't forget the tonic I prepared for you. You have to protect your voice."

"You and your homemade remedies."

"They work, don't they?"

"Yes, maman," said Stephanie and kissed her mother on the cheek.

Roseline was so proud of Stephanie. Roseline couldn't sing a note to save her life and now Stephanie was attending the University of Miami on a music scholarship. With Roger's help, the musical director of the church had trained Stephanie and made the opportunity possible.

Roseline felt indebted to Roger and he took advantage of this. Despite paying Roseline below the minimum wage, Roger expected a meal from her on the last Friday of every month.

"My doctor says this food is too rich for me—what with my high blood pressure," said Roger as he ran his stubby fingers along Roseline's arm. "But god damn, you sure know how to cook."

Roseline, like the other women janitors who were illegals, tolerated Roger's behavior. For although Roger was an elder, he wasn't below calling immigration on any woman who didn't comply with his demands, which included a code of silence.

Roger used a similar tactic with Stephanie.

"If you breathe a word to your mother, little girl, it's back to Haiti."

But when Roseline found Stephanie crying in the bathroom, she cradled her in her arms and rocked her to sleep. Then, using what she had learned from Alcide, Roseline nursed Stephanie back to health and made sure that Stephanie never took the blame for Roger's evil.

"I don't want you to be here when he comes," Roseline said. "With the strength of the women who came before us, we'll pretend as if nothing happened."

But Roger was going to pay. And if Jesus couldn't do it, then the loas would.

Once Stephanie left, Roseline sprinkled a special seasoning over the meal she had prepared. Made from puffer fish, it contained just enough neurotoxins so Roger could make it home to his wife where it would seem as if he had had a stroke.

The doorbell rang. It had to be Roger. Right on time.

"One minute," Roseline said and took off her wedding band.

"Roger," she said and opened the door. "So good to see you. Everything's set."

Geoffrey Philp is the author of the novel "Garvey's Ghost", and is currently working on a poetry collection entitled "Letter from Marcus Garvey." He lives in Miami, teaching English at the Inter-American Campus of Miami Dade College

THE BEST
TIPS ARE
BENEATH
THE SURFACE

...discover them in the LOST iN mobile app

LOST iN